GROUNDCOVER
SERIES

Text research: Richard Ashby

Acknowledgements

I am grateful to many people for their contributions in the making of this book.
In particular I wish to thank Richard Ashby for his researching skills and Les Birchall
who so enthusiastically shared his knowledge of his home city. My appreciation also
extends to Steve Bremner, Chris Britain, Father Denis Clinch, Angela Dixon, Simon Paine,
Bernadette Potts, Robert Reddaway, John Ryland's Library, Elaine Simpson, Steve Simpson,
and David Taylor and the staff of Manchester Central Library, Archives and Local Studies.

Photographs of Chetham's Hospital and Library are reproduced with the kind permission
of the Governors, and the photograph of Ordsall Hall is reproduced with the kind
permission of the City of Salford Museum and Heritage Services.

Credit belongs to Malcolm Crampton for suggesting this title, and special thanks go to
Caroline Jarrold, Sarah Letts, Geoffrey Sutton, Kaarin Wall and all at Jarrold Publishing.

John Curtis

Front cover picture: Chepstow Street
Back cover picture: The Lowry, Salford Quays

Designed and produced by
Jarrold Publishing,
Whitefriars, Norwich NR3 1TR

All photographs
© John Curtis
except page 93 (Ordsall Hall)
© City of Salford Council

© Jarrold Publishing 2002

ISBN 0-7117-2077-0

Printed in Belgium.

1/02

PUBLISHER'S NOTE
Variant and archaic spellings have
been retained in quoted material,
while the modern spellings of
place-names have been used in
headings.
    The inclusion of a photograph
in this book does not necessarily
imply public access to the building
illustrated.

MANCHESTER

JOHN CURTIS

JARROLD
publishing

Royal Exchange

MANCHESTER

GROUNDCOVER
SERIES

Castlefield

Contents

MANCHESTER SHIP CANAL
WARBURTON

The impressive scale of the enterprise and the engineering aspects of this massive project have bedazzled generations of historians and commentators who have seen the Ship Canal as epitomizing those qualities of hard work, heroism and supreme self-confidence which have been considered attributes of nineteenth century Manchester.

IAN HARFORD *Manchester and its Ship Canal Movement: Class, Work and Politics in Late Victorian England* 1994

Introduction

Manchester is arguably England's second city; some Victorian commentators, influenced by the radical innovations for which the city was already famous, were moved to place it first. More than once Manchester has been referred to as the first 'shock city', and Benjamin Disraeli, after a visit in 1843, described it as 'the most wonderful city of modern times'.

An important centre for communications – the Romans built a fort to protect river crossings here – with easy access to coal supplies, combined with the exploitation of water power and high humidity, Manchester quickly became a world leader in the development of textile industries. The spread of canals and railways, in particular the opening of the Manchester Ship Canal in 1894 giving direct access to the sea and making it the country's third port, further contributed to the rapid growth of manufacturing and commerce. 'What Manchester did yesterday, England does today and the world follows tomorrow' ran a local saying.

Always forward-looking, Manchester today is one of England's most successful business locations. The university campus is one of the largest in Europe, and the city centre has undergone a renaissance with exciting new and refurbished apartments, hotels, restaurants, cafés, bars and public spaces. Mancunians are famed for their love of sport, and the sporting facilities here, many specially built for the 2002 Commonwealth Games, are second to none.

A walk around the city centre will reveal that Manchester has also been careful to preserve much of its illustrious past. The area round the largely fifteenth-century cathedral and Chetham's Hospital remains a quiet oasis away from the bustle of city life, while magnificent Victorian warehouses, mills and commercial buildings, many with striking Italianate façades, have been restored and appear fresh and new. Towering over all is Alfred Waterhouse's gothic Town Hall of 1869, one of the greatest architectural monuments of Victorian Britain. Numerous museums, art galleries and theatres make Manchester the cultural capital of the North. In neighbouring Salford, Salford Quays is excitingly redeveloped with offices, shops and houses along with the internationally acclaimed Lowry and Imperial War Museum.

Around Manchester, and all within easy access, are many other interesting towns and villages, stately homes, historic sites and unspoilt countryside.

Photographing Manchester and its environs proved to be a particularly stimulating and ultimately rewarding challenge. I hope that the following images capture something of the contrasting aspects of this unique and dynamic city.

JOHN CURTIS

ALBERT MEMORIAL

There are few royal statues in Manchester – only the Prince Consort in Albert Square and Queen Victoria in Piccadilly. The others are local dignitaries or Liberal statesmen… Achievement is what matters in Manchester, not a historic name or a cultivated accent.

A.J.P. TAYLOR
Manchester
1957

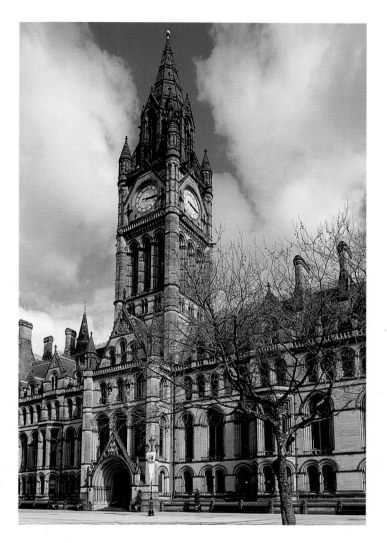

TOWN HALL

Manchester is essentially a Victorian city, and if one can only lift one's eyes from the pavements, there is Architecture worth seeing. *Quod erat demonstrandum.*

CECIL STEWART
The Stones of Manchester
1956

TOWN HALL (LEFT) AND ALBERT SQUARE (RIGHT)

One day in my pre-occupations I walked down a public lavatory in Albert Square and discovered myself in the Ladies' reserve; and an old woman who was in charge threw up her hands at the sight of me and 'shoo'd' me out saying, 'Get away from here, you impudent young rascal!' A more unjust suspicion than this has never been levelled at anybody since the world began.

NEVILLE CARDUS
Autobiography
1947

LIBRARY WALK

… the curved walk between the Library and the Extension is a wonderfully exciting piece of townscape with a touch of ominous mystery that keeps its thrill from becoming too familiar.

MICHAEL KENNEDY *Portrait of Manchester* 1970

CENTRAL LIBRARY
ST PETER'S SQUARE

That as in this institution special provision has been made for the working classes, by means of a free lending library, this meeting cherishes the earnest hope that the books thus made available, will prove a source of pleasure and improvement in the cottages, the garrets, and the cellars of the poorest of our people.

Resolution moved by Charles Dickens and seconded by William Thackeray at the opening of the Free Library, Manchester
2 September 1852

Manchester's first public library opened in 1852. For a time it was housed in the old Town Hall in King Street and then in temporary buildings in Piccadilly until it moved to the new Central Library in 1934.

ST PETER'S SQUARE

St Peter's Square is partly on the site of St Peter's Fields where, on 16th August 1819, a large crowd gathered to press for 'the most LEGAL and EFFECTUAL means of attaining REFORM in the Commons House of Parliament'. The Riot Act was read and in the charge of the Hussars and Manchester Yeomanry that followed eleven demonstrators were killed and over 500 injured. The Massacre of Peterloo has entered history as a milestone on the road to a free and democratic England.

TOWN HALL EXTENSION

The building's bold simplicity … was almost too much for Manchester at the time, though it was this that enabled it to make a successful transition between the Town Hall's elaborate Gothic and Library's Classical style, without overpowering or compromising either.

PHILIP ATKINS
Guide across Manchester:
a Tour of the City Centre
including the Principal Streets
and their Buildings.
1976

MIDLAND HOTEL
PETER STREET

The Stones of Manchester, together with the bricks and terracotta trimmings, which are heaped up in monumental confusion at the sides of the streets, are nearly all the product of the Victorian age; for Manchester, however distant its origins, survives today as a memorial to Victorian building enterprise.

CECIL STEWART *The Stones of Manchester* 1956

FREE TRADE HALL
PETER STREET

It is interesting to note, as A.J.P. Taylor has pointed out, that whereas other cities might have halls named after a public personality or saint, Manchester's chief hall was dedicated to a proposition. Above all, it was a monument, and the site on which it stood was the site not only of the triumphs of the [Anti-Corn Law] League but of the Massacre of Peterloo.

ASA BRIGGS
Victorian Cities
1963

BARBIROLLI SQUARE

Manchester is changing. Of course it is. It's a continuing process. Cities and towns are like other structures of human organisation, they are always changing. Nothing stands still. If a city does not move forward boldly into the future it slips back towards decay.

GEORGE MOULD
Manchester Memories
1972

BRIDGEWATER HALL

I have heard the crash of
    ancient buildings
    falling,
And, above the dust
    and roar,
I can hear the city's voice
    in music calling
To the years that lie
    before.

ARTHUR BENNETT
From 'The City of My Dream'
1928

GREATER MANCHESTER EXHIBITION AND EVENT CENTRE (G-MEX)

Urban redevelopment can be imaginative. The conversion of the redundant Central Station into the Greater Manchester Exhibition Centre (G-Mex) is an example of what can be done to redesignate rather than demolish the city's industrial and commercial heritage.

ALAN KIDD
Manchester
1996

MANCHESTER INTERNATIONAL CONVENTION CENTRE

It's the city that has suddenly sprung to international recognition… At last, the *Evening Standard*'s teeshirts claiming 'There Is No Life North Of Watford' are gathering dust while shirts emblazoned with the message that 'On The Eighth Day God Created MANchester' are selling like Eccles Cakes.

DEBBIE RIDEHALGH AND MIKE PARKER
The Raw Guide to Greater Manchester
1991

CITYSCAPE

Manchester is acquiring a reputation of a town of some architectural character; it is the inland metropolis of the North … it has developed a style of architecture which we may largely call our own, and in which we may take a not unnatural pride.

THOMAS WORTHINGTON
Presidential Address to the Manchester Society of Architects
1875

'PEVERIL OF THE PEAK'
CHEPSTOW STREET

… its was believed to have been founded by a character called Grundy who drove one of the busy Manchester to London stage coaches in the days before the railways arrived. His particular coach was known as the 'Peveril of the Peak' and Grundy is thought to have pocketed many of the coach fares himself, providing the finances to establish the pub.

NICK BURTON *Exploring Manchester: Historical Strolls around the City Centre* 1996

ROCHDALE CANAL

The streets of Manchester are as true a record of the ideals and shortcomings of Victorian society as any historical document. A century of change and decay has failed to destroy the essential character of the city …

ANTHONY J. PASS
Thomas Worthington: Victorian Architecture and Social Purpose
1988

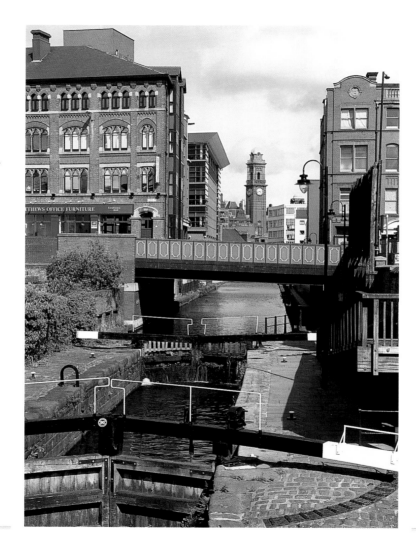

METRO LINK

Approach Manchester by any form of transport and you may well say 'this is no mean city'. It is my city. I love it.

GEORGE MOULD
Manchester Memories
1972

LOCK 92,
DUKE'S LOCK
CASTLEFIELD

Today Castlefield basin and
the canals that feed it are being
slowly and painfully saved
from the final dereliction of
over-development … Beautiful
Victorian buildings that would
once have been destroyed
are being converted into
accommodation, offices, bars
and restaurants, and a kind of
linear urban park is being
created that threads the very
heart of Manchester.

MIKE HARDING
*Tales from the Towpath: a Canalside
Ramble through Central Manchester*
1992

MERCHANT'S
BRIDGE
CASTLEFIELD

It is in a unique and inspirational
location, which is Britain's first
industrial heritage site, and for
engineers very much part of
their history.

Built over the Bridgewater
canal at its junction with the
Rochdale canal, the bridge is set
amongst bridges: fifteen are
visible from the structure.

MARK WHITBY
In *Sites of the City: Essays on Recent
Buildings by their Architects*
1996

CASTLEFIELD VIADUCT

This is the true beginning of Manchester, its history is all around you. Here was the Roman fort and the small Saxon town that superseded it. Here the pioneering Bridgewater Canal brought the coal that fuelled the industrial revolution and the agricultural produce that fed the workers. Here were built the warehouses to store the products of the factories for despatch by the canals and it was here that the first railway station, the terminus of the Manchester and Liverpool Railway, was opened in 1930.

ROMAN FORT
CASTLEFIELD

When Pliny lost his life, and Herculaneum was buried, Manchester was born. Whilst lava and ashes blotted from sight and memory fair and luxurious Roman cities close to the Capitol, the Roman soldiery of Titus, under their general Agricola, laid the foundations of a distant city which now competes with the great cities of the world.

Mrs G. Linnæus Banks *The Manchester Man* 1896

LIVERPOOL ROAD STATION

Opened in 1830, Liverpool Road Station is the earliest-surviving passenger station in the world. The separate entrances for first- and second-class passengers, first class being larger and more imposing, are an interesting reminder of early nineteenth-century class distinctions.

LIVERPOOL ROAD

In proportion to its size and population, Manchester boasts a larger number of educational establishments than any town in the Kingdom; and if Manchester men have proved themselves apt in commercial and trading pursuits, they may with equal justice lay the claim to high praise for their persevering and untiring endeavours to promote the comfort and education of the thousands they employ.

G.F. PARDON *The Manchester Conductor: a Guide to Visitors to the Great Art Treasures' Exhibition* 1857

THE MUSEUM OF **SCIENCE** AND **INDUSTRY** IN MANCHESTER

The size and prosperity of the city have been brought about through the aid of several inventions, notably of steam and cotton machinery, but above all by the industry and commercial spirit of its inhabitants.

Manchester, Salford and District ('Our own District' Series)
1911

ST JOHN'S GARDEN

… of late, the Town hath been much improved by the building of many fair and stately Houses; which make a very handsome Street.

WILLIAM CAMDEN
Britannia: or a Chorographical Description of Great Britain and Ireland together with the adjacent lands
1722

ST JOHN STREET

The large and populous town of *Manchester*, has now excited the attention and curiosity of strangers, on account of its extensive trade, and the rapid increase of its buildings, with the enlargement of its streets …

A Description of Manchester, Giving an Historical Account of those Limits in which the Town was formerly included … by a Native of the Town
1783

FORMER GREAT NORTHERN RAILWAY WAREHOUSE
DEANSGATE

Manchester, like England, is now re-creating itself, looking for a new role, a life without manufacturing industry.

DAVE HASLAM
Manchester, England: the Story of the Pop Cult City
1999

The exterior of many of the Manchester warehouses and places of business are very imposing and, in some instances, beautiful.

Manchester as it is: or, Notices of the Institutions, Manufactures, Commerce, Railways etc of the Metropolis of Manchester …
1839

ST MARY'S CHURCH
MULBERRY STREET

Herbert Vaughan became the second Bishop of Salford in 1872. In 1892 he became the Cardinal Archbishop of Westminster. He had a special love for St Mary's, Mulberry Street … [and] used to say that 'No matter on what side of the church you look, you behold a hidden gem.' From then on, by Episcopal designation, as it were, St Mary's became known as *The Hidden Gem*. The church's hidden position has given further meaning to the Vaughan title.

DENNIS CLINCH
Manchester's Hidden Gem: a Celebration in Words and Pictures of St Mary's Mulberry Street, The First Two Hundred Years, 1794–1994

MIDLAND BANK
KING STREET

Native pride alone does not sponsor the assertion that it is the most famous of provincial cities, indeed that it is *the* provincial city.

MICHAEL KENNEDY
Portrait of Manchester
1970

FORMER BANK OF ENGLAND
KING STREET

In Manchester, this famous town,
  What great improvements
    have been made, sirs;
In fifty years 'tis mighty grown
  All owing to success in trade,
    sirs;
For see what mighty buildings
    rising,
  To all beholders so surprising,
The plough and harrow are now
    forgot sirs,
  'Tis coals and cotton boil the
    pot, sirs.
  Sing Ned, sing Joe, sing Frank,
    so gaily,
  Manchester's improving daily!

Mid-nineteenth-century ballad

MANCHESTER ART GALLERY
MOSLEY STREET

The Manchester Art Gallery
contains a collection of very
beautiful pictures, among which
are to be found works by most of
the best modern English painters.
They are hung in well-warmed,
well-lighted rooms, and may be
visited without payment, so that
all who care for beautiful things
may see them constantly, and
learn to love and value them.

The Story of Lancashire
1896

FORMER REFORM CLUB
KING STREET

Manchester is a more interesting city to walk over than London. One can scarcely walk about Manchester without coming across frequent examples of the *grand* in architecture. There has been nothing to equal it since the building of Venice.

Building News 20 January 1861

FORMER LOMBARD CHAMBERS AND BROOKS'S BANK
BROWN STREET

… this place has preserved, through successive ages, its rank amongst the first of the British towns; in many of the great political events which have marked the eras of our national history, it has taken a prominent part; the first of the staple manufactures of the kingdom has chosen this for its favourite seat; and the capability displayed by Manchester at the present moment for future growth exceeds even its past prosperity.

EDWARD BAINES
History, Directory, and Gazetteer of the County Palatine of Lancaster
1825

SHIP CANAL HOUSE
KING STREET

… a Lancashire village has expanded into a mighty region of factories and warehouses. Yet, rightly understood, Manchester is as great a human exploit as Athens.
The inhabitants, indeed, are not so impressed with their idiosyncrasy as the countrymen of Pericles and Phidias. They do not fully comprehend the position which they occupy. It is the philosopher alone who can conceive the grandeur of Manchester, and the immensity of its future.

BENJAMIN DISRAELI
Coningsby: or the New Generation
1844

ST ANN'S CHURCH
ST ANN'S SQUARE

The font of this church is only second to that of the Collegiate church in the number of children baptized. And, if such a phrase may be decorously allowed, on so sacred a subject, it has been the fashion for the more respectable inhabitants of the town, ever since the consecration of Saint Ann's church, to take their children thither, for baptism, in preference to any other.

The Manchester Guide: a Brief Historical Description of the Towns of Manchester and Salford, the Public Buildings and the Charitable and Literary Institutions
1804

EXCHANGE THEATRE
ROYAL EXCHANGE

After more than a century and a half of trading in cotton came to an end in the 1960s, the idea of using the space available for a theatre marks another imaginative new use for a building which has outlived its original purpose. Its remarkable design enables all 700 members of the audience to be no more than 30ft away from the stage area.

MR THOMAS'S CHOP HOUSE
CROSS STREET

The name of this institution could be straight out of a Dickens novel and the distinctive brick and terracotta building was once the haunt of Dickensian businessmen slurping chops and supping ale.

NICK BURTON *Exploring Manchester: Historical Strolls around the City Centre* 1996

JOHN RYLAND'S LIBRARY
DEANSGATE

… an … exquisite example of Arts and Crafts Gothic … with its marvellous spaces, extraordinary atmosphere, and lovely detail.

JAMES STEVENS CURL
Victorian Architecture
1990

The building and its adornments are in them-selves one of the sights of the city: it is quite the best modern building in Manchester …

Black's Guide to Manchester
1909

HIGH COURT OF JUSTICE AND CROWN COURT
CROWN SQUARE

Post-war planning would have seen the destruction of a large swathe of central Manchester for the creation of a new 'processional way' focused on the Town Hall. Fortunately most of the scheme was abandoned and only the surprisingly distinguished Crown Court, built in 1962, survives as a monument to such discredited policies.

OPERA HOUSE
QUAY STREET

[Manchester] … is large enough and sufficiently renowned to command the best in all spheres of civilized life, yet compact enough to hold the affection of a civic community in an atmosphere of pleasing intimacy. This is the heritage which the sons and daughters of Manchester will do well to cherish.

Rich Inheritance: a Guide to the History of Manchester 1962

TRINITY BRIDGE

Amongst the many recent
developments in Manchester
have been a number of new
bridges of stunning design.
Perhaps the most spectacular is
Trinity Bridge, spanning the
River Irwell, which provides a
new link between Salford and
Manchester City Centre.

KENDAL'S DEPARTMENT STORE
Deansgate

The luxury shops are in Deansgate,
St. Ann's Square and King Street,
and this is the principal district
for the buying of clothes.
Here may be seen a thousand
temptations and enticements.

Manchester Civic Week.
Official Handbook
1926

ARNDALE BRIDGE
CORPORATION STREET

The terrorist bomb that destroyed much of the commercial heart of Manchester in 1996 opened up numerous possibilities for redevelopment and refurbishment of a much wider area. Manchester, as always, responded with vigour and has created a new and exciting cityscape from the devastation.

BARTON ARCADE
DEANSGATE

Kits of parts provided scope for elaborate designs using cast iron: shop-fronts were often of this material. These kits could provide anything from a *pissoir* to an exportable church, but the ingenuity of design enabled elaborate structures to be fitted into difficult sites, as at the Barton Arcade, Deansgate, Manchester. Cool in summer and protected in the winter, arcades were planned with shops in the ground floor, while often galleries on the upper floors would lead to offices. At the Barton Arcade the detail, all mass-produced, is wonderfully put together …

JAMES STEVENS CURL
Victorian Architecture
1990

MANCHESTER CATHEDRAL

The church of Manchester was
apostolic – that is, everything
goes in twelves: twelve clerestory
windows in choir and nave,
twelve bays, twelve altars, and so
twelve stalls on each side of the
choir with niches for twelve times
twelve saints, which, however,
seem never to have been
placed in them.

E.F. LETTS
*Lancashire and Cheshire Archaeological
Society's Transactions*
1886

MANCHESTER CATHEDRAL

Here – 'mid the tumult of
the street and mart,
There rises sheer above
the busy ways
This dream of Piety fulfilled
by Art –
Rock-like amid the surge
– a House of Praise.

THOMAS CRUDDAS PORTEUS
From 'Manchester Cathedral'
1905

THE CHETHAM LIBRARY
CHETHAM'S HOSPITAL

The Chetham Library at Manchester is the true Mecca of the free endowed library. Humphrey Chetham, an example of the 'Manchester Man' at his best … died in 1653, leaving in his will £1000 'for or towards a library within the town of Manchester, for the use of scholars and others well affected … The same books there to remain as a publick librarie for ever.' The door of the Chetham library has never been closed since …

L. STANLEY JAST
The Library and the Community
1939

CHETHAM'S HOSPITAL

Nothing more impresses the stranger visiting Manchester than to pass from the busy hum of the City through the gate of the Chetham Hospital to the peaceful quiet of its cloistered court, oak screened dining hall, and quaintly panelled rooms.

ALBERT NICHOLSON *The Chetham Hospital and Library with the Historical Associations of the Building and its Former Owners* 1910

The buildings now accommodate the Chetham's School of Music

CHETHAM'S HOSPITAL

The foundation, was originally for forty poor boys, who were to be clothed and educated, from the age of six to fourteen, when they were to be put apprentice… They are fed with a plain but wholesome diet, and their countenances bespeak the kindness they are treated with.

The Manchester Guide: a Brief Historical Description of the Towns of Manchester and Salford, the Public Buildings and the Charitable and Literary Institutions
1804

OLD WELLINGTON INN
EXCHANGE SQUARE

Now, I am willing to confess that I was ignorant, wholly ignorant, till I beheld the scene, that MANCHESTER dines at ONE!!! Rich, poor, ignorant, learned, Destructive, Conservative, Dissenter, Churchman – the mass – yes, the mass, all dine at one!!

Blackwoods Edinburgh Magazine
April 1839

EXCHANGE SQUARE

Renowned … for its indomitable spirit for, just four years after a massive terrorist bomb struck its very heart, a new city centre has risen Phoenix-like from the ashes of the devastation. Cosmopolitan, welcoming and more accessible, with stylish squares and pleasant open spaces, the new look city centre has even more to offer Manchester residents, workers and its many millions of visitors.

MANCHESTER CITY COUNCIL
Building a better future
2000

VICTORIA STATION

A charming Edwardian buffet stands amongst the bustle of the refurbished Victoria Station, redolent of a more gracious era of travel by train.

CIS OFFICES
MILLER STREET

These impressive tower blocks … dramatically herald the entrance to the city centre for motorists approaching over Ducie Bridge. The discipline and care put into their design, that made them the best of the office blocks that transformed the city skyline in the 1960s, leaves them looking crisp and good today, unlike many others.

PHILIP ATKINS
Guide across Manchester: a Tour of the City Centre including the Principal Streets and their Buildings.
1976

ROYAL MILL
REDHILL STREET

A modern observer can see that Manchester was the first predominantly industrial city in the history of the world. No other town had ever been so much given over to the demands of the factory system. And in no other town had the techniques of production by steam-powered machinery ever been applied so extensively.

GARY MESSINGER
Manchester in the Victorian Age: the Half Known City
1985

Back of GEORGE LEIGH STREET

Ancoats

Dora went to live in Ancoats
… which lies but a stone's-
throw from the principal
thoroughfares and buildings
of Manchester, and in its
varieties of manufacturing
life and population presents
types which are all its own.
… Manchester is a city with
a common life, which
London is not.

Mrs Humphrey Ward
The History of David Grieve
1892

ANITA STREET Ancoats

… the street was a showcase for the Manchester city fathers because every single house contained proper internal plumbing, an untold comfort for labourers in the cotton mills. The city fathers proclaimed their pride in the name of the street: Sanitary Street. Later inhabitants, uneasy at having their bowel movements trumpeted to the world, insisted on dropping the first and last letters.

Jeremy Paxman *The English* 1998

Former DAILY EXPRESS BUILDING GREAT ANCOATS STREET

… the most modern of all, the Daily Express building, Great Ancoats Street … all glass and black *Vitrolite* and rounded corners, and almost identical to [Sir Owen Williams'] Fleet Street building. But then, Manchester was still the greatest regional newspaper publisher, and still home to the *Manchester Guardian*.

John Parkinson-Bailey
Sites of the City: Essays on Recent Buildings by their Architects
1996

GATEWAY HOUSE PICCADILLY STATION APPROACH

One of Manchester's better 1960s buildings. Its pleasing serpentine shape recalls the long-abandoned plans for a major traffic interchange below the station approach.

CROWN COURT
MINSHULL STREET
FORMER POLICE AND
SESSIONS COURT

The style of the building will
be of that type of the Pointed
Gothic of which examples
abound in Florence, Sienna,
Pisa, Verona, and the other
cities of the north of Italy.

The Builder
18 July 1868

LEVER STREET

The new streets built within these
few years have nearly doubled the
size of the town. Most of them are
wide and spacious, with excellent
and large houses, principally of
brick made on the spot; but they
have a flight of steps projecting
nearly the breadth of the
pavement, which makes it very
inconvenient to foot passengers.
When two people meet one must
either go into the horse road, or
over the flight of steps, which in
the night time is particularly
dangerous, as the lamps are not
always lighted.

JOHN AIKIN
*A Description of the Country from Thirty
to Forty Miles round Manchester*
1795

BRITANNIA HOTEL
PORTLAND STREET

The Britannia occupies what was once one of Manchester's finest warehouses, built for drapers S. & J. Watts, opened in 1858 and designed in an extravagant imitation of the grand *palazzi* of Renaissance Italy. Host in its time to everybody from Frankie Goes to Hollywood to Madonna, the Britannia Hotel, by the middle of 1995, was trading on these associations; 'Hang out with the rock stars' trumpeted its publicity material …

DAVE HASLAM
Manchester, England: the Story of the Pop Cult City
1999

LANCASTER HOUSE
WHITWORTH STREET

Life is returning to the heart of Manchester. Living in fashionable apartments in former warehouses or offices has proved so appealing that by the Millennium up to 10,000 people had already moved back into the city centre.

CANAL STREET

When I was a student in Manchester I walked for miles all over the city just looking and staring and savouring the exciting air of what was, and still is, my home town… It was a city that I got to know through the leather of my shoes… I remember it as a magical place, full of echoes and atmosphere …

MIKE HARDING *Tales from the Towpath: a Canalside Ramble through Central Manchester* 1992

CHINA TOWN

Manchester is recognised as a 'Dragon City'. It has the largest Chinese community in the country outside London, centred in a thriving and vibrant Chinatown where, in 1987, Europe's first imperial Chinese arch was built by twelve craftsmen from the People's Republic itself.

CHINA TOWN

New life has been brought to the narrow streets of the area by the provision of shops and supermarkets, banks and medical and educational facilities serving the many people who visit or who now live in the newly converted residential accommodation, and at lunchtime and in the evenings the many restaurants are busy with lovers of Chinese cuisine.

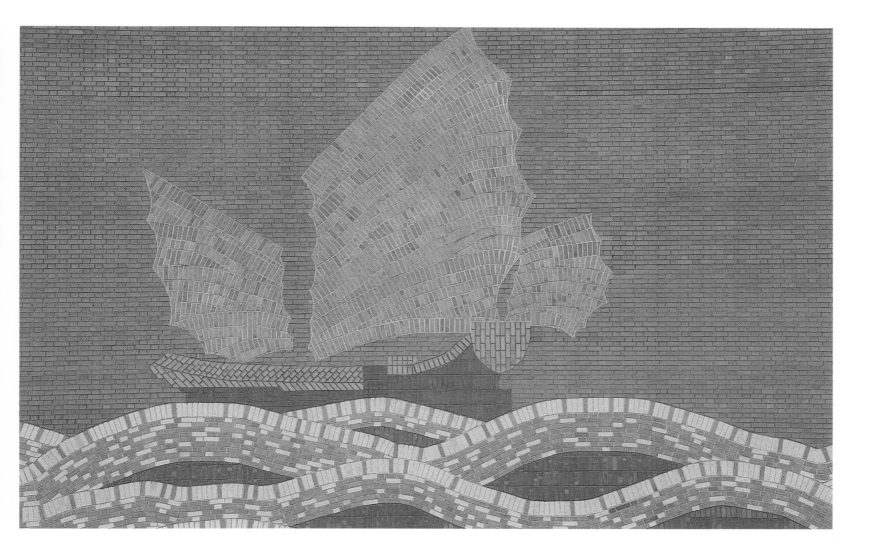

Former REFUGE ASSURANCE BUILDING
Oxford Street

In every great business centre there are numerous insurance offices. Manchester can boast of plenty… They possess some very fine buildings, but the Refuge Office in Oxford Street, against the railway arch, promises to be the finest of all. It is an immense place, beautifully built. Its topmost tower is said to be as high as the Town Hall Tower.

Manchester, Salford and District ('Our own District' Series)
1911

The Refuge Assurance building is now converted into the Palace Hotel.

HOME OF EMMELINE PANKHURST
72 NELSON STREET

… the city has this further characteristic of a capital that it is an active manufactory of agitation and thought. It is the headquarters of the temperance movement and the vegetarian movement, and indeed harbours as many living causes as Oxford does lost ones.

Manchester in 1915; being the Handbook for the Eighty-Fifth Meeting of the British Association for the Advancement of Science held in Manchester September 7–10, 1915

MANCHESTER UNIVERSITY
OXFORD ROAD

In the ancient world commerce and culture had gone hand in hand, and Manchester had followed that great example in founding her University and offering to her industrial people that education in the arts and sciences which had become a monopoly of the well-to-do in the ancient universities.

J.L. HAMMOND
C.P. Scott, 1846–1932: the Making of the Manchester Guardian
1946

MANCHESTER AQUATICS CENTRE
OXFORD ROAD

Built for the 2002 Commonwealth Games, the new pool provides another world-class facility for the people of Manchester.

Former SALFORD TOWN HALL
Bexley Square

The many great improvements that have been made in the towns of Manchester and Salford within the last ten years, surpass belief. The numerous and splendid public structures for devotion, charity, pleasure and business; the immense range of newly-erected dwelling-houses, distributed into streets and squares, in the most eligible situations, and in a style of superior elegance … exhibits at one view the effects of industry directed by genius, and supported by public spirited and benevolent characters …

A Concise Description of Manchester and Salford
1826

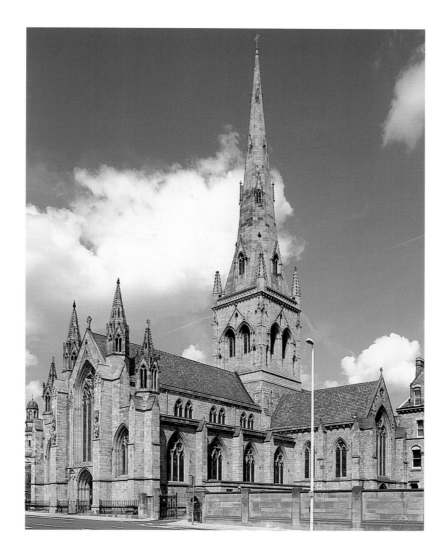

SALFORD CATHEDRAL

Many Victorian church architects drew their inspiration from medieval examples, but here in Salford is a blatant hybrid where the nave, choir and tower have been copied from three different churches. Nevertheless the eminent Victorian architect A.W.N. Pugin approved of the result.

THE LOWRY
FOOTBRIDGE
SALFORD QUAYS

The Plan seeks to create a new quarter of the City which has a unique character derived from the way in which all parts of the development are related to water. Some places within the Quays should be vast and urban with almost continual public activity on the water and the water's edge. Other places should be very closed-in secluded places, where the public may enter (only by foot), but where they feel the privacy of others must be respected.

*Salford Quays: Development Plan
for Salford Docks*
1985

SALFORD QUAYS

Perhaps we, who were born into a mere acceptance of the accomplished fact, do not realize how marvellous the thing is; this creation of the fourth port of the Kingdom on a spot where a country house and estate stood within the memory of men not yet much more than middle-aged.

The Soul of Manchester 1929

IMPERIAL WAR MUSEUM (NORTH)
SALFORD QUAYS

The underlying concept for the
museum will be the 'shattered globe'
of the fragile Earth whose shards
represent the cultures and lives lost
and destroyed in global conflict.

DAVID HANDS AND SARAH PARKER
Manchester: a Guide to Recent Architecture
2000

THE LOWRY
SALFORD QUAYS

… its place on the Manchester Ship Canal is
historically significant because it engages with a
time when the Canal was a gateway for
traditional heavy industries and a 'corridor of
opportunity'. Now it can be again, in a new era
of creativity and media. A different age, a
different trade, but a new beginning for Salford.

JEREMY MYERSON
Making The Lowry
2000

THE VICTORIA
HARBOUR CITY, SALFORD QUAYS

The changes which have taken place in and about Manchester since I first drew breath … have been many and great. The advance, whether it be civic, commercial, political or philanthropic, has been steady, rapid and material.

LOUIS M. HAYES
Reminiscences of Manchester and Some of its Local Surroundings from the Year 1840
1905

ORDSALL HALL
ORDSALL LANE, SALFORD

The legend that Ordsall Hall was the location for Guy Fawkes and Robert Catesby to plot the overthrow of King James in what was to become the famous Gunpowder Plot was popularised in the novel by the Victorian author Harrison Ainsworth. Such has been the credibility of the legend that the street directly adjacent to the hall has been named 'Guy Fawkes Street'.

MANCHESTER UNITED FOOTBALL GROUND
OLD TRAFFORD

Until my dying day I shall be grateful to Manchester United for all that my association with the club has given me. For somebody who loves football as much as I do, there is no better place to be.

ALEX FERGUSON
Managing my Life
1999

BARTON AQUEDUCT

Brindley's Barton Aqueduct had no precedent in Britain: the spectacle it presented, of boats on the canal passing high in the air over barges on the river, immediately caught the imagination of the public and it became famous.

P.J.G. RANSOM *The Archaeology of the Transport Revolution, 1750–1850* 1984

The present swing bridge, which replaced Brindley's aqueduct in 1893, is itself still an engineering wonder.

TRAFFORD CENTRE

Three miles of shop fronts

280 retail units

30 restaurants and bars

1,600-seat food court

20-screen cinema

2 million facing bricks

1.9 million sq feet (176,500 sq m)
    of space

484,000 sq feet (45,000 sq m) of
    Italian granite and marble

43 hydraulic lifts

19 escalators

WORSLEY

… the enterprising spirit and astonishing perseverance of the Duke of Bridgewater, who, unassisted, except by the natural genius of Brindley, carried into execution a series of difficult and expensive works, which are, even at this time, unexampled.

The primary object of 'The Father of British Inland Navigation,' as the Duke of Bridgewater has been styled, was to open his valuable collieries at Worsley, and to supply the town of Manchester with coal at a much cheaper rate than could be done by the imperfect navigation of the Mersey and Irwell.

JOSEPH PRIESTLY
Historical Account of the Navigable Rivers, Canals, and Railways of Great Britain
1831

LYMM CROSS

It is founded on a rock. The very streets of the town are cut out of it, and their stone houses gather round the stocks and a huge cross, its steps crowned with a massive stone cupola and a sundial, its base hewn from the rock.

ARTHUR MEE
The King's England: Cheshire
1968

HALL I' TH' WOOD
BOLTON

The oldest Lancashire manor house par excellence… [Here] Samuel Crompton invented the spinning mule which revolutionized the textile industry and laid the foundations for Lancashire's C19 prosperity, now alas dissipated. [It] was rescued in 1899 by 1st Viscount Leverhulme.

JOHN MARTIN ROBINSON *A Guide to the Country Houses of the North West* 1991

HEATON HALL
HEATON PARK

Heaton-house, the seat of lord Grey de Wilton, about four miles from Manchester, is beautifully situated on an eminence in a rich park highly manured and well wooded… The apartments are truly noble, and fitted up in the first style of elegance… From the temple in the park is a most delightful view over an extensive and well-wooded country.

JOHN AIKIN
A Description of the Country from Thirty to Forty Miles round Manchester
1795

SADDLEWORTH MOOR

I remember Saddleworth as a place where, at certain moments, a generally dull landscape broke for short periods into vivid life. Spring was always a disappointment; I always missed the mighty surge of growth of other places. It was always late, and always brief. But late summer, when the cotton grass bloomed in the bogs, was beautiful because of it; and autumn was unique …

GLYN HUGHES
Millstone Grit
1975

CO-OPERATIVE STORE
TOAD LANE, ROCHDALE

Hard times often gave the unscrupulous the opportunity to exploit their fellow men. A pernicious system of 'Tick Shops' grew up in many districts. Rochdale had its share. Out of this emerged the Rochdale Pioneers, who determined to beat the exploiters… Since 1844 when the first co-operative shop was started, the system has spread far and wide.

MARY LUTY
Some Rochdale Worthies
1955

MANCHESTER JEWISH MUSEUM
CHEETHAM HILL ROAD

There has been a thriving Jewish community in Manchester for the past 200 years. Its story is told in the Manchester Jewish Museum housed in the former Spanish and Portuguese Synagogue, built in 1874 and the oldest surviving synagogue building in the city. The congregation initially comprised some thirty families only, some 200 people, but nevertheless the building was distinguished by fine Moorish architecture and splendid stained glass, all now lovingly restored.

MORAVIAN SETTLEMENT
FAIRFIELD

The Moravian Socialist Establishments have not failed, and why? because they were undertaken in the fear of God, and with humility and caution, because the Moravians have believed, and acted up to their own creed, and that they were brothers and sisters, members of one body, bound to care not for themselves but for the common weal.

CHARLES KINGSLEY
The Application of Associate Principles and Methods to Agriculture
1851

CITY OF MANCHESTER STADIUM (LEFT) AND NATIONAL CYCLING CENTRE (RIGHT)

More spectacular architecture has resulted from the development of venues for the 2002 Commonwealth Games. They remain a priceless asset for the people of Manchester, not only in the provision of world-class sporting and recreational facilities but also as a symbol of the energy and commitment made to the regeneration of Manchester as a twenty-first-century city.

GREAT UNDERBANK
STOCKPORT

The most charming of [the old houses] is in the old street called Great Underbank; used now as a bank, this splendid old home of the Arderne family is a gracious example of timbering, delightfully patterned, with a porch, an overhanging storey, and three gables.

ARTHUR MEE
The King's England: Cheshire
1968

STOCKPORT VIADUCT

This structure presents one of the most imposing works of the kind in the kingdom, whether viewed as to its general design or exquisite workmanship. It is in the highest degree interesting to the civil engineer; and will long remain a monument of the skill of him who designed it, and of the energy and perseverance of those who were entrusted with its execution, and have so successfully brought it to completion.

FRANCIS WISHAW *The Railways of Great Britain and Ireland: Practically Described and Illustrated* 1840

PEAR NEW MILL
LOWER BREDBURY

Greater Manchester is widely renowned as one of the great centres of the Industrial Revolution. It is associated in particular with the cotton industry, as first Manchester and later other towns within the modern county developed mass production methods in textile mills of huge scale.

MIKE WILLIAM AND D.A. FARNIE *Cotton Mills in Greater Manchester* 1992

BRAMALL HALL
BRAMHALL

A warrior rode through the
    beechen woods,
And by the elm trees tall
And on the glistening casements
    gazed
Of Bramhall's gabled hall.

Bathed in a mellow golden light
The noble old house stood;
Its framework all of massive oak,
Its carvings rich and good.

'Now, never a fairer house
    than this
Have I seen this many a day;
Fit hall for a courteous knight,
    I wis,
Fit bower for a lady may.'

JOHN LEIGH
From 'The Maid of Bramhall Hall'
1880

LYME PARK
DISLEY

… we … come to Lime; the stately seat and scituation whereof, with the large spacious Park richly stored with Red and Fallow Deer, with all other fitnesse for Lordly delights, may well shew the worthy discent of that great Family and name of the Leighs of Lyme, of whom, though there have been many famous Knights, and renowned Owners, yet none more compleat and accomplished in generous and heroical virtues, then Sir Peter Leigh, now Possessor thereof, a noble Gentleman, and of great respect.

WILLIAM WEBB
Vale Royal of England
1656

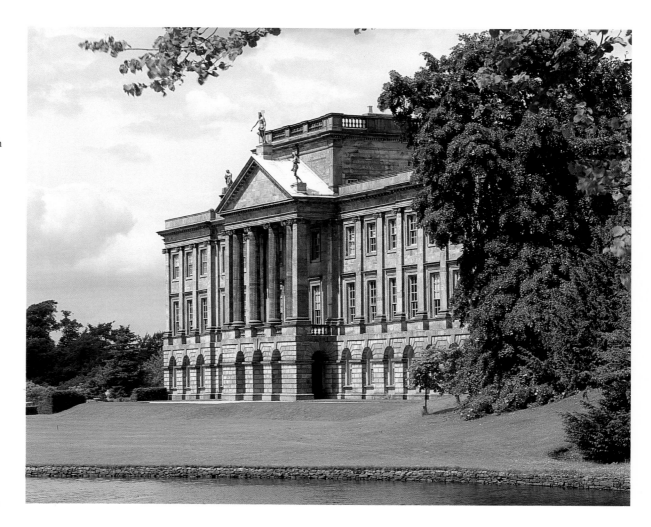

STYAL WOODS
(LEFT)
AND QUARRY BANK MILL
(RIGHT)

The superiority of rural over urban manufacture, is a conclusion, not only deduced from reasoning, but … a matter of experience also… The proprietors of these establishments rank high as intelligent and benevolent men, and their conduct to their operatives, during a period distinguished by many commercial and political changes, is a fact which reflects the greatest honour upon their country.

L. FAUCHER
Manchester in 1844
1844

TATTON PARK
KNUTSFORD

Few places can give such a vivid insight into the contrasting lives of its residents as Tatton. The magnificent mansion and its contents are much as they were in the time of the Egerton family, who lived there for nearly 400 years and who created the house and park we see today. Alongside the state rooms the servants' quarters provide an interesting insight to life below stairs. In the park are splendid and varied gardens, terraces, lawns, herbaceous borders and a Japanese garden. The rhododendrons and azaleas are famous.

DUNHAM MASSEY
ALTRINCHAM

… *Dunham Massey*, the seat of the earl of Stamford … is seated in the midst of an extensive park, full of fine timber, the unmolested growth of many years, through which avenues or vistas are cut, affording views of the hall… This noble family have long afforded to the country an instructive example of the virtues by which rank and fortune are made truly useful and respectable.

JOHN AIKIN
A Description of the Country from Thirty to Forty Miles round Manchester
1795

DUNHAM MASSEY
ALTRINCHAM

A pleasant road brings us to Dunham Massey park, with deer roaming among its 400 acres… In one of its most charming corners is an old water-mill with a great wheel under an arch.

ARTHUR MEE
The King's England: Cheshire
1968

Wythenshawe Hall

Acknowledgements

Every effort has been made to secure permissions from copyright owners to use the extracts of text featured in this book.

Any subsequent correspondence should be sent to Jarrold Publishing at the following address: Jarrold Publishing, Whitefriars, Norwich NR3 1TR.

page
13 (left) 'Manchester' by A.J.P. Taylor. By kind permission of the publisher.
13 (right) *The Stones of Manchester* by Cecil Stewart. By kind permission of Edward Arnold (Publishers) Ltd.
15 *Autobiography* by Neville Cardus. By kind permission of Harper Collins Publishers.
16 (bottom) *Portrait of Manchester* by Michael Kennedy. By kind permission of Robert Hale Ltd.
19 (right) *Guide across Manchester …* by Philip Atkins. By kind permission of The Civic Trust for the North West.
20 (bottom) As for page 13 (right).
20 (right) *Victorian Cities* by Lord Asa Briggs. By kind permission of the author.
23 (left) *Manchester Memories* by George Mould. By kind permission of Terence Dalton Ltd, Suffolk.
24 (left) *Manchester* by Alan Kidd. By kind permission of Edinburgh University Press.
24 (right) *The Raw Guide to Greater Manchester* by Debbie Ridehalgh and Mike Parker. By kind permission of Chambers Harrap Publishers.
27 (bottom) *Exploring Manchester: Historical Strolls around the City Centre* by Nick Burton. By kind permission of the author and Sigma Press.
28 (left) *Thomas Worthington: Victorian Architecture and Social Purpose* by Anthony J. Pass. By kind permission of the author.
28 (right) As for page 23 (left).
31 (left) *Tales from the Towpath: a Canalside Ramble through Central Manchester* by Mike Harding. Manchester City Council.
31 (right) 'Merchants Bridge' by Mark Whitby. By kind permission of the author.
40 (left) *Manchester, England: the Story of the Pop Cult City* by Dave Haslam. By kind permission of HarperCollins Publishers.
43 (left) *Manchester's Hidden Gem…* by Fr Dennis Clinch. By kind permission of the author.
43 (right) As for page 16 (bottom).
51 (bottom) As for page 27 (bottom).
52 (left) *Victorian Architecture* by Prof. James Stevens Curl. By kind permission of the author.
55 (bottom) *Rich Inheritance: a Guide to the History of Manchester*. Manchester City Council.
59 (right) As for page 52 (left).
63 (left) *The Library and the Community* by L. Stanley Jast. By kind permission of Nelson Thornes Ltd.
67 (left) *Building a better future*. Manchester City Council. Burroughs Communications Ltd.
68 (left) As for page 19 (right).
68 (right) *Manchester in the Victorian Age: the Half Known City* by Gary Messinger. By kind permission of Manchester University Press.
71 (bottom) *The English* by Jeremy Paxman. By kind permission of David Higham Associates Ltd.
72 (left) *Sites of the City: Essays on Recent Buildings by their Architects*. By kind permission of the editor.
76 As for page 40 (left).
79 (bottom) As for page 31 (left).
84 (top) *C.P. Scott, 1846–1932: the Making of the Manchester Guardian* by J.L. Hammond. Frederick Muller.
88 (right) *Salford Quays: Development Plan for Salford Docks*. By kind permission of Salford City Council.
91 (top) *Manchester: a Guide to Recent Architecture* by David Hands and Sarah Parker. By kind permission of Elipsis.
91 (bottom) *Making The Lowry* by Jeremy Myerson. By kind permission of The Lowry.
95 (top) *Managing my Life* by Alex Ferguson. Reproduced by permission of Hodder & Stoughton Ltd.
95 (bottom) *The Archaeology of the Transport Revolution, 1750–1850* by P.J.G. Ransom. By kind permission of the author.
99 (right) *The King's England: Cheshire* by Arthur Mee. © The estate of Arthur Mee and The King's England Press Ltd.
100 (bottom) *A Guide to the Country Houses of the North West* by John M. Robinson. By kind permission of Constable & Robinson Ltd.
103 (top) *Millstone Grit* by Glyn Hughes. By kind permission of the Mic Cheetham literary agency.
103 (bottom) 'Some Rochdale Worthies' by Mary Luty. By kind permission of Lancashire Life.
109 (left) As for page 99 (right).
118 (right) As for page 99 (right).

Bibliography

Editions and dates in this bibliography are those of the items that have been examined. In some cases earlier editions have significant differences to those listed here.

Aikin, John: *A Description of the Country from Thirty to Forty Miles round Manchester.* John Stockdale, 1795.

Atkins, Philip: *Guide across Manchester: a Tour of the City Centre, including the Principal Streets and their Buildings.* Civic Trust for the North West, 1976.

Baines, Edward: *History, Directory, and Gazetteer of the County Palatine of Lancaster.* Vol. II, Wm. Wales & Co., 1825. Reprinted by David & Charles.

Banks, Mrs G. Linnæus: *The Manchester Man.* Abel Heywood & Sons, 1896.

Bennett, Arthur: 'The City of My Dream' in *Contemporary Lancashire Poetry.* Fowler Wright, 1928.

Black's Guide to Manchester, ed. Joseph E. Morris. 14th ed., Adam & Charles Black, 1909.

The Bridgewater Hall: International Orchestra & Celebrity Recitals. Opening Season. Bridgewater Hall, [1996].

Briggs, Asa: *Victorian Cities.* Odhams Press, 1963 and Penguin Books, 1968.

The Builder. Vol. xxvi, no.1328, 18 July 1868.

Building News. 20 January 1861.

Burton, Nick: *Exploring Manchester: Historical Strolls around the City Centre.* Sigma Press, 1996.

Camden, William: *Britannia: or a Chorographical Description of Great Britain and Ireland together with the adjacent lands.* 2nd ed., James & John Knapton et al., 1722.

Cardus, Neville: *Autobiography.* Collins, 1947.

Clinch, Dennis: *Manchester's Hidden Gem: a Celebration in Words and Pictures of St Mary's Mulberry Street, The First Two Hundred Years, 1794–1994.* St Mary's Church, Mulberry Street, [1992].

A Concise Description of Manchester and Salford, Containing an Account of their Antiquities, Public Buildings &c., compiled from the Most Authentic Records. Leek & Cheetham, 1826.

Curl, James Stevens: *Victorian Architecture.* David & Charles, 1990.

Dickens, Charles: 'Resolution moved by Charles Dickens and seconded by William Thackeray at the opening of the Free Library, Manchester. 2 September 1852' in *The Speeches of Charles Dickens*, ed. K.J. Fielding. Clarendon Press, 1960.

A Description of Manchester, Giving an Historical Account of those Limits in which the Town was formerly included … by a Native of the Town. C. Wheeler, 1783.

Dickens, Charles: 'The speech of Charles Dickens at the annual meeting of the Institutional Association of Lancashire and Cheshire, 3 December 1858' in F.R. Dean: *Dickens and Manchester.* The Dickens Fellowship, reprinted from *The Dickensian*, March 1938.

Disraeli, Benjamin: *Coningsby: or the New Generation.* 5th ed., 1849. Heron Books, [nd].

Faucher, L.: *Manchester in 1844.* London, 1844.

Ferguson, Alex: *Managing my Life: my Autobiography.* Alex Fergusson with Hugh McIlvaney. Hodder & Stoughton, 1999.

Hammond, J.L.: *C.P. Scott, 1846–1932: the Making of the Manchester Guardian.* Frederick Muller, 1946.

Hands, David and Parker, Sarah: *Manchester: a Guide to Recent Architecture.* Elipsis, 2000.

Harding, Mike: *Tales from the Towpath: a Canalside Ramble through Central Manchester.* Central Manchester Development Corporation, 1992.

Harford, Ian: *Manchester and its Ship Canal Movement: Class, Work and Politics in Late Victorian England.* Ryburn Publishers, Keele University Press, 1994.

Haslam, Dave: *Manchester, England: the Story of the Pop Cult City.* Fourth Estate, 1999.

Hayes, Louis M.: *Reminiscences of Manchester and Some of its Local Surroundings from the Year 1840.* Sherrat & Hughes, 1905.

Hughes, Glyn: *Millstone Grit.* Victor Gollancz, 1975.

'In Manchester, this famous town …' in *Black's Guide to Manchester*, ed. Joseph E. Morris. 14th ed. Adam & Charles Black, 1909.

Jast, Stanley L.: *The Library and the Community.* Thomas Nelson & Sons, 1939.

Kennedy, Michael: *Portrait of Manchester.* Robert Hale, 1970.

Kidd, Alan: *Manchester: Town and City Series.* 2nd ed., Keele University Press. 1996.

Kingsley, Charles: 'The Application of Associate Principles and Methods to Agriculture. J.J. Bezer, 1851' in *Fairfield – a Moravian Settlement.* Dissertation for a BA Hons. by James L. Birchall, 1970.

John Ryland's Library, Deansgate

Leigh, John: *Lays and Legends of Cheshire with other poems & ballads.* John Heywood, 1880. Republished by E.J. Morten, 1972.

Letts E.F.: *Lancashire and Cheshire Archaeological Society's Transactions.* Vol. IV, p. 130, 1886, in *Black's Guide to Manchester*, ed. Joseph E. Morris. 14th ed. London, Adam & Charles Black, 1909.

Luty, Mary: 'Some Rochdale Worthies' in *Lancashire Life.* Vol. III, no. 10, Spring 1955.

Manchester as it is: or, Notices of the Institutions, Manufactures, Commerce, Railways etc of the Metropolis of Manchester … Manchester, Love and Barton, 1839. Reprinted E.J. Morten, 1971.

Manchester City Council: *Building a better future.* Burroughs Communications, 2000.

Manchester Civic Week. Official Handbook. Manchester Civic Week Committee, 1926.

Manchester in 1915; being the Handbook for the Eighty-Fifth Meeting of the British Association for the Advancement of Science held in Manchester September 7–10, 1915. Manchester University Press, 1915.

Manchester, Salford and District ('Our own District' Series) Edward Arnold, 1911.

Mee, Arthur: *The King's England: Cheshire.* First publ. 1938, ed. E.T. Long. Hodder & Stoughton, 1968.

Messinger, Gary S.: *Manchester in the Victorian Age: the Half Known City.* Manchester University Press, 1985.

Mould, George: *Manchester Memories.* Terence Dalton, 1972.

Myerson, Jeremy: *Making The Lowry.* The Lowry Press, 2000.

Nicholson, Albert: *The Chetham Hospital and Library with the Historical Associations of the Building and its former Owners.* Sherrat & Hughes, 1910.

Pardon, G.F.: *The Manchester Conductor: a Guide to Visitors to the Great Art Treasures' Exhibition.* J. Hampson, 1857.

Pass, Anthony J.: *Thomas Worthington: Victorian Architecture and Social Purpose.* Manchester Literary and Philosophical Publications, 1988.

Paxman, Jeremy: *The English.* Michael Joseph, 1998, and Penguin Books, 1999.

Porteus, Thomas Cruddas: 'Manchester Cathedral' in *A selection of verse from the Manchester University Magazine 1868–1912, with a preface by Sir Alfred Hopkins.* Manchester University Press, 1913.

Priestly, Joseph: *Historical Account of the Navigable Rivers, Canals, and Railways of Great Britain.* Longman, Rees, Orme,

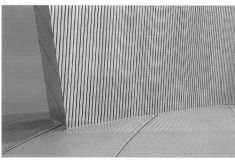

The Imperial War Museum

Brown & Green, 1831. Reprinted by David & Charles, 1969.

Ransom, P.J.G.: *The Archaeology of the Transport Revolution, 1750–1850.* Kingswood, 1984.

Rich Inheritance: a Guide to the History of Manchester, ed. N.J. Frangopulo. Manchester Education Committee, 1962.

Ridehalgh, Debbie and Parker, Mike: *The Raw Guide to Greater Manchester.* Harrap Books, 1991.

Robinson, John Martin: *A Guide to the Country Houses of the North West.* Constable, 1991.

The Rochdale Equitable Pioneers' Society: an Illustrated Souvenir. Cooperative Union, 1967.

Salford Quays: Development Plan for Salford Docks. Salford City Council, 1985.

Saturday Review of Politics, Literature, Science, and Art. Vol. 121, no. 3140, p. 19, 1 January 1916.

Sites of the City: Essays on Recent Buildings by their Architects, ed. John Parkinson-Bailey. Faculty of Art and Design, Manchester Metropolitan University, 1996.

The Soul of Manchester, ed. W.H. Brindley. Manchester University Press, 1929.

Stewart, Cecil: *The Stones of Manchester.* Edward Arnold (Publishers), 1956.

The Story of Lancashire. Edward Arnold, 1896.

Taylor, A.J.P.: 'Manchester' in *Encounter.* Vol. III, no. 3, March 1957.

Ward, Mrs Humphrey: *The History of David Grieve.* 6th ed., Smith, Elder, 1892.

Webb, William: 'Vale Royal of England, 1656' in *The House of Lyme from its Foundation to the end of the Eighteenth Century by the Lady Newton.* William Heineman, 1917.

'A Week at Manchester' in *Blackwoods Edinburgh Magazine.* No. cclxxii, vol. xlv, April 1839.

Wishaw, Francis: *The Railways of Great Britain and Ireland: Practically Described and Illustrated.* John Weale, 1840.

Worthington, Thomas: 'Presidential Address to the Manchester Society of Architects' in *Thomas Worthington: Victorian Architecture and Social Purpose.* Manchester Literary and Philosophical Publications, 1988.

Manchester Evening News Arena

Index

GROUNDCOVER
SERIES